PERFORMANCE
EDITIONS

THE BAROQUE ERA
Early Intermediate Level

Compiled and Edited by Richard Walters

AUDIO ACCESS INCLUDED
Recorded Performances Online

Recorded by

Elena Abend
Matthew Edwards
Stefanie Jacob
Christos Tsitsaros
Jeannie Yu

To access companion recorded performances online, visit:
www.halleonard.com/mylibrary

Enter Code
3237-8152-8253-0512

On the cover:
The Allegory of Painting (1666)
by Johannes Vermeer (1632–1675)

ISBN 978-1-4803-3818-0

G. SCHIRMER, *Inc.*

DISTRIBUTED BY

HAL•LEONARD®
CORPORATION
7777 W. BLUEMOUND RD. P.O. BOX 13819 MILWAUKEE, WI 53213

www.musicsalesclassical.com
www.halleonard.com

CONTENTS

Though the table of contents appears in alphabetical order by composer, the music in this book is in progressive order.

The price of this publication includes access to companion recorded performances online, for download or streaming, using the unique code found on the title page. Visit **www.halleonard.com/mylibrary** and enter the access code.

The music in this collection has been edited by the compiler/editor Richard Walters, except for the pieces previously published in other volumes in the Schirmer Performance Editions series:

Anonymous: Minuet, BWV App. 116; Musette, BWV App. 126;
Minuet, BWV App. 132
from *First Lessons in Bach*
edited and recorded by Christos Tsitsaros

C. P. E Bach: March, BWV Appendix 122
from *First Lessons in Bach*
edited and recorded by Christos Tsitsaros

Petzold: Minuet, BWV App.114; Minuet, BWV App. 115
from *First Lessons in Bach*
edited and recorded by Christos Tsitsaros

COMPOSER BIOGRAPHIES
AND
PERFORMANCE NOTES

General Comments about the Baroque Era and This Edition

As is the case with many Baroque pieces, we often do not have dynamics and articulations from the original composer. This music was not written with a modern piano in mind. The harpsichord and claviers of the period were not capable of dynamic variation in the manner of a modern piano. When playing Baroque music on the piano it is only natural to add dynamic contrasts, which makes it more idiomatic for the modern instrument. Dynamics and articulations have been added as editorial suggestions in many instances.

Minuet is traditionally spelled differently, depending on the language. For this edition we have chosen to use the traditional English spelling "minuet." One might encounter some of the minuets in this collection elsewhere with various spellings in various languages: Minuet (English); Minuetto (Italian); Menuet (French); Menuett (German).

A minuet was a dance movement, originating in France, usually in 3/4 meter, popular in the period between 1650–1800. It has regular four measure phrases and is in binary form. In a classic minuet that is to be danced, the second beat of the measure is accented. However, composers do not always observe this. Minuets became concert music inspired by dance music, but not intended for dancing. The minuet was one of the only Baroque dance music forms that survived into the Classical Era.

In the Baroque period, ornamentation is part of the style and was historically added by players in the performance. In this edition intended for students, we have been very discreet in any ornament suggestions. However, a teacher might guide a student in adding ornamentation. Ornamentation can be heard sometimes on the companion recording which may be used as a guide.

A constantly applied *legato* touch, common to piano playing after the Romantic period, is not appropriate to music of the Baroque and Classical periods. *Legato* playing should be deliberately chosen only for specific places, such as the notes included in a slur, not generally applied as a default. Style in the Baroque period comes from maintaining steady rhythm, a crisp touch with careful attention to articulation, the general avoidance of the sustaining pedal, and period ornamentation. In most instances a slightly separated touch, *portato*, should be applied when no articulation is indicated.

Because the notes below are likely to be read one piece at a time as needed, many concepts applying generally to playing Baroque period music are restated many times.

ANONYMOUS

Johann Sebastian Bach included the following pieces (BWV Appendix 116, 126, 132) in the second volume, dated 1725, of the *Notebook for Anna Magdalena Bach*. The notebooks (the first was begun in 1722) were for Bach's second wife, Anna Magdalena, who was much younger than the composer. Such keyboard notebooks of assembled favorite pieces were common in Baroque homes, and used for family music-making. (They are the equivalent of the modern published music collection, such as this one.) Some of the pieces in the Anna Magdalena notebook are by J.S. Bach; others are not. Previously attributed to Bach, we now know that the pieces below are not J.S. Bach compositions. The composers are unknown. We can assume that they date from the first decades of the eighteenth century and are likely German in origin.

Minuet in G Major, BWV Appendix 116

The music is in three large sections, ABA. The A section is measures 1–16; the B section moves to the minor key beginning in measure 17; measure 33 begins a repeat of measures 9–16. You would do well to consider that the notes that are not marked with phrasing should be played slightly separated. This will help capture Baroque style. As is true of most music of this period, this piece should be played with absolutely steady rhythm and no pedal. We have no tempo from the composer. The companion recording offers a good suggestion of a standard tempo of this minuet.

Musette in D Major, BWV Appendix 126

A musette was a small French bagpipe in the seventeenth and eighteenth centuries. A musical piece called a musette is dance music with a melody idiomatic for the musette (imagine an oboe playing the melody line), over a bass line drone. The dance-like quality of this music requires a steady beat throughout without deviation in tempo. We have no tempo marking from the unknown composer, but the companion recording is an excellent guide, offering a tempo that many would accept as a standard one for this piece. Play with no pedal. The bouncing octaves of the left hand, which appear almost throughout, should be played with a light staccato touch. The left hand sometimes interrupts its octave bounce accompaniment by playing with the right hand in different places, such as in measures 3–4. Articulation and dynamics are editorial suggestions. To find Baroque style it is recommended that you play any notes not marked with slurs as slightly detached. In a quicker tempo piece, such as this, playing with a detached touch is, in practical terms, *staccato*. Slurs indicate that the notes within the slur should be played *legato*. This is a simple ABA form (not considering the repeats). The B section is measures 9–20.

Minuet in D Major, BWV Appendix 132

There are four slurs, indicated by the asterisks in this edition, which appear in the source manuscript. The rest of the slurs are stylistic editorial suggestions. Dynamics also are editorial suggestions since none appear in the source manuscript. The left hand notes should be played with slight separation, except in places where there are marked slurs, which indicate that the group of notes within the slur should be played *legato*. Fundamental to the style of the piece is playing different articulations in each hand. You might choose to play the repeat of the first eight measures at a softer dynamic. A technical challenge that needs attention is in the right hand in measures 10 and 12. Moving down the tenth and back up gracefully and quickly will take some practice. The short two-note phrases in measure 5 in the right hand are easily overlooked, but are an important stylistic component of the Baroque.

CARL PHILIPP EMANUEL BACH
German composer.
Born in Weimar, March 8, 1714;
died in Hamburg, December 14, 1788.

Carl Philipp Emanuel Bach, second son of Johann Sebastian Bach, was a major composer bridging the distinctions between late Baroque and early Classical periods, writing in the *empfindsamer Stil* (sensitive style), meaning an emotionally turbulent or dynamically expressive compositional style, distinguished from the more restrained rococo. Carl received music lessons from his father until he began studies in law at Leipzig University and continued in Frankfurt. After graduation,

C.P.E. Bach accepted a position in the court orchestra of Crown Prince Frederick of Prussia and moved to Berlin. In 1768 C.P.E. Bach became the music director of sacred music for the city of Hamburg, a position previously held by his godfather, Georg Philipp Telemann. C.P.E. Bach was extraordinarily prolific, writing over 1,000 works for voices and keyboard instruments.

March in D Major, BWV Appendix 122

This march, included in the second volume of the *Notebook for Anna Magdalena Bach*, is usually attributed to Carl Philipp Emmanuel Bach. A march, generally in 2/2 meter, needs a very steady beat. When deciding on a tempo for a march, imagine a walking tempo. In this case it is a rather quick walk, with a quarter note equal to each step. (The companion recording offers an excellent guide for a tempo suggestion.) Because there are no articulations and dynamics in the original manuscript, we have made stylistic suggestions. In addition to this, an insightful player of Baroque style will note that the notes not marked with slurs should be played detached, such as the quarter notes in measures 1–3 and the eighth notes in measures 8 and 21. Measures 8 and 21 are a military trumpet call accompanied by the low repeated bass note, implying a military drum. Many times in piano music, to achieve bounce and evenness, one alternates fingers on repeated notes. However, because of the quick tempo, the repeated bass notes in measures 8 and 21 might be best played with one finger, rather than by alternating fingers.

JOHN BLOW
English composer, organist, and teacher.
Born in Newark, February 23, 1648 (or 1649);
died in London, October 1, 1708.

Blow was a choir boy at the Chapel Royal in London until his voice changed. He excelled at organ and composition and in 1668 became organist for Westminster Abbey. He was granted various other prominent court and church titles, including Master of the Children of the Chapel, Composer-in-Ordinary for Voice in the Private Music, Organist for the Chapel Royal, and Master of the King's Music. Such a lofty and public career put him in contact with the best British musicians of his day. He was a contemporary of the other great British composer of his time, Henry Purcell. Blow composed an enormous amount of choral music, much of which was written for specific occasions, songs, organ pieces and works for harpsichord. His opera *Venus and Adonis* is among the first operas by a major composer in the English language.

Courante in C Major

A courante (the French word is translated as "current") is a Baroque dance movement in triple meter with origins in the Renaissance. A courante became part of the standard Baroque suite, following the allemande in traditional suite order. Though there were international variations in how a courante was written in various parts of Europe, it usually has a melody over a simple accompaniment, and that is the case in this example. We have made stylistic suggestions for articulations which will help find some lively style in this graceful piece. Carefully execute the *staccatos*, which alternate with the slurred notes. Trills in the Baroque period begin on the note above the principal note. Thus, the trill in measure 3 begins on G; the trill in measure 12 begins on B. The *allegretto* tempo marking is an editorial suggestion, since there is no tempo marking from the composer. This piece requires elegance and lightness of touch, and should be played with no pedal.

Prelude in C Major

The constant sixteenth note movement of this prelude is common to the Baroque Era. Steadiness and evenness are the most important musical qualities of a performance of music such as this. Tempo must be strictly kept, with no variance in the beat. If you have done diligent work practicing scales, this piece will reward that effort. This prelude, and many other Baroque pieces like it, is not particularly about dynamic contrasts. Playing the relentless sixteenth notes evenly is much more important than imposing artificial changes of dynamics on this music. The two places where some dynamic variation is appropriate are at the end of the first section in measure 9, and in the last measure of the piece. The left hand quarter notes should be played slightly detached throughout. You will probably want to begin with a slow tempo as you practice hands separately. Increase the speed gradually over several weeks of practice as you master the music, but maintain a steady tempo whatever speed is taken. Like many other major key *allegros*, there is a bubbly, happy quality about this music.

FRANÇOIS COUPERIN

French composer, harpsichordist, and organist.
Born in Paris, November 10, 1668;
died in Paris, September 11, 1733.

François was the son of the organist at Saint Gervais church in Paris. His father died when the boy was ten. Saint Gervais not only saved his father's position for the budding young musician and paid for his musical education, the church also paid for the housing and upkeep of François and his mother until he was old enough to assume the duties as full-time organist in 1688. In this period the royal court controlled all copyrights. Couperin obtained permission to publish his music. He was appointed organist of the King in 1693 and began teaching harpsichord to much of Parisian aristocracy. For the rest of his life he was regarded as one of the greatest teachers and keyboard players in France. Couperin published four books of harpsichord pieces, considered as landmarks of the French Baroque style. He was the author of a definitive treatise, *The Art of Harpsichord Playing*, addressing fingering, touch, ornamentation and various other aspects of keyboard technique.

Berceuse (Les graces-naturéles)
from the eleventh order of Harpsichord Pieces, Book 2

French Baroque music often requires a refined touch. That is certainly the case with this piece. There are often three voices at play. One is the treble melody; another is the quarter note bass voice (marked with downward stems); the third is the filler voice of eighth notes in between the treble and bass voice. The presence of three voices is not constant. (Often in piano music, voices drop out and re-enter.) The form of the piece is A (measures 1–4 and its repeat), B (measures 4–12, with a repetition in measures 12–16), C (measures 16–24), and then a return to A and B. Typical of the period, the composer did not indicate articulation and dynamics, relying on the player's knowledge of the expected style. The two-note slur followed by two *staccato* notes is a common stylistic characteristic in Baroque music. In our articulation suggestions we have indicated this pattern, such as in measures 1, 2, 3, and other similar places. Paying careful attention to articulation and playing without pedal will help you find the appropriate style. In general, play notes not marked with articulation with slight separation, such as the quarter notes in the left hand in measure 11.

Benevolent Cuckoos Under Yellow Dominos
from *French Follies, or Costumes at a Masked Ball*
from the thirteenth order of Harpsichord Pieces, Book 1

This movement is the tenth of twelve variations from a set written as political satire on the moral state of France. Each movement was characterized by various domino masks (a small rounded mask covering only the eyes) at a masquerade party. "Yellow Dominos" in the title therefore meant bird characters in yellow masks. We can only guess at what the composer meant by "benevolent" as part of his satire. However, one does not need to understand the original context and political meaning to enjoy this lovely piece, which asks for a delicate touch. We have suggested some articulation intrinsic to Baroque style, generally adding *staccato* markings on eighth notes. In measure 1 and similar places, the left hand chord in the first beat needs to lift and clear precisely on beat 2. In the right hand in measure 1, notice that beat 3 is a sustained note, not *staccato*, and needs to clear exactly on beat 1 of the next measure. Such attention to detail will give your playing rhythmic crispness. The most difficult challenge in the piece, beyond achieving its steady delicacy, is the stylistic trill on beat 3 in the left hand of measure 7. This trill was in the composer's original score. We have made it optional in brackets because of is difficulty. One might instead choose to play only the trills in the right hand. Use no pedal in this playing this piece.

LOUIS-CLAUDE DAQUIN
French composer, harpsichordist, and organist.
Born in Paris, July 4, 1694;
died in Paris, June 15, 1772.

A child prodigy, Daquin studied with his mother and at the age of six played the harpsichord for King Louis XIV. Two years later he was conducting his own compositions at the Sainte-Chapelle. At age twelve he became organist at a convent, the beginning of a series of high profile organist positions, including the Chapelle Royale, St. Paul's, Notre Dame, and Cordeliers. Daquin was considered one of the greatest keyboard players and improvisers of his time. He published much keyboard music, chamber music, and vocal music, much of which is lost.

The Cuckoo (Le Coucou)
from Harpsichord Pieces, Book 3
The cuckoo is ever-present in this lovely French Baroque piece. We hear the call of the cuckoo almost immediately in the left hand. The right hand takes on the cuckoo's call on the second page, in measures 23–30. This music requires a delicate touch. A pianist needs to play with refined but firm tone and absolute steadiness and evenness. We strongly suggest practicing hands alone. Only after you master the notes and can achieve steadiness should you move on to a quicker tempo. This piece not only asks that one plays quickly, but also quietly. Rhythmic precision is paramount. Notice that the half notes in measures 1–3, for instance, should be released precisely on beat 3. The same is true in measures 5–9. In our editorial suggestions of style, at some places in the left hand the fourth note of a measure is *staccato*, such as in measures 1–3; in other places we have suggested a slur from beat 4 to beat 1, such as in measures 5–9. If you cannot master the tempo that is on the companion recording, find a tempo that is comfortable for you and that you can play well. In faster music, make sure that your tempo is steady and sounds under control. Guard against the common mistake of speeding up during the piece.

WILLIAM DUNCOMBE
English composer and organist.
Born in 1736 (or 1738);
died in 1818 (or 1819).

Very little is known about the life of Duncombe. He served as the organist in the London district of Kensington. Apart from the handful of short pedagogical works, such as the Sonatina in C Major and an often-heard fanfare, his music is now unknown.

Sonatina in C Major
A sonatina was a form that evolved from the Baroque into the Classical Era. The early use of this term did not have the same meaning that became common in the Classical Era. In the Baroque period "sonatina" simply indicated a short instrumental work. Typical of the Baroque period, the composer did not add articulations. We have made articulation suggestions that will help find some of the Baroque style in performance. The quarter notes in the left hand, such as in measures 4–7, should be played slightly detached. If you make no attempt at articulation and style, this little piece runs the risk of being dull. However, applying style through crisp articulation creates something lovely. Notice the two-note slurs in measure 7, a characteristic of the period. Also notice the two-note slur followed by two staccato notes in measures 9–14, also characteristic of the period. This music needs to be played steadily and without pedal.

GEORGE FRIDERIC HANDEL
German composer.
Born in Halle, February 23, 1685;
died in London, April 14, 1759.

Handel was one of the defining composers of the Baroque period. After a brief time in Italy as a young man, he spent nearly his entire adult career in London, where he became famous as a composer of opera and oratorio, including *Messiah*, now his most recognizable music. Handel also wrote numerous concertos, suites, overtures, cantatas, trio sonatas, and solo keyboard works. Though he taught some students early in his career and occasionally instructed members of the London aristocracy, Handel was not known for his teaching abilities. His keyboard works were likely not written for any of his students, but to fulfill commissions or generate income. Handel composed various keyboard works until 1720, when he became master of the orchestra for the Royal Academy of Music, an organization dedicated to performing new operas. After Italian opera fell out of vogue in London, Handel turned his compositional efforts to oratorio.

Impertinence (Bourrée), HWV 494
A bourrée is a lively dance movement, French in origin, from the Baroque. A bourrée is in 2/2 or 4/4 meter, in binary form (meaning in two sections), and always begins with a quarter note upbeat. A bourrée became an optional part of the standard Baroque suite. Though it fell out of favor after the Baroque period among

composers, the original folk dance is still found in the Auvergne region of France. There will be liveliness and style in your performance if you make some attempt at crisp articulation. We have made stylistic suggestion of articulations (since these were not provided by the composer), indicating staccato notes and brief slurs of no more than a few notes. The trills in measures 7 and 19 should begin on the note above. This music needs to be played with steadiness and a delicate touch. Practice hands alone at a slow tempo, confirming fingering and adding articulation in the early stages of practice. Then practice hands together at a slow tempo, retaining the articulation already learned. As you become more comfortable with the music, gradually increase the tempo, but retain steadiness at whatever tempo you are playing. The tempo marking Vivace is open for interpretation. One can imagine that it may be played more quickly than that on the companion recording. Whatever tempo you choose, it must remain steady throughout and cannot rush. There is wit in Handel's title of "Impertinence," indicating an irreverent rebel.

Minuet in F Major

This is quite a courtly little minuet. Imagine aristocracy of the eighteenth century dancing gracefully in a candle-lit ballroom wearing powdered wigs and finery. Any minuet is all about style. If one plays only the notes on the page with no consideration to articulation and finesse, the result will be pedestrian and uninteresting. But if one pays attention to style, using the suggested Baroque articulation, there can be a sparkling result. Your playing must have clarity, steadiness and evenness of tone. Quarter notes not marked as staccato, such as in the left hand in measures 4, 12, 16, etc., should be played slightly detached, not as short as *staccato*. It is a mistake when pianists apply *legato* as a default norm in Baroque and Classical styles. The many trills, which add enormously to the style, should all begin on the note above. In measure 2 the small notes that precede beat 3 (called an "escape") come at the end of the trill, just before the next note.

Rigaudon in G Major

A rigaudon, similar to a bourrée, is a folk dance from southern France that became popular in the French court at the end of the seventeenth century, and spread to Germany and England. A rigaudon is usually happy music in a major key, with simple phrase structure and binary form. Like most Baroque music (which was written not for a modern piano, after all) a pianist should use no pedal. We make stylistic recommendation that the left hand should be played slightly detached throughout. This is not as short as true *staccato*. Play as if these quarter notes were notated as eight notes followed by eighth rests. The right hand

has completely different articulation from the left hand. In this edition, we have suggested small groups of notes to be slurred. The two-note slurs in measures 2–3, 12–13, and 14–15 are particularly fun to play. Do not make the mistake of applying general *legato* touch to playing Baroque music. The trills (measures 7, 10 and 19) should begin on the notes above the principle note, which is always true in the Baroque and Classical periods. Tempo is always subjective. The *allegretto* tempo might be taken a little more quickly than the performance on the companion recording.

Sarabande from Suite in D minor, HWV 437

The sarabande has its roots in the zarabanda, a fast and erotic dance from Mexico and Spain in the sixteenth century. In France, the zarabanda was transformed into a slow Baroque dance, the sarabande, essentially a highly expressive slow minuet. Baroque sarabandes tend to be either majestic or mournful, and are musically characterized by a dotted note on the second beat of a three beat measure. This particular sarabande is a theme with variations. In the theme, the quarter notes in the left hand should be played slightly detached, appropriate to Baroque style. The half notes also should be played slightly detached. The repeat of the theme (page 1 of the music) is optional, as are the repeats of variations 1 and 2. The repeats are included on the companion recorded because we need to responsibly record the content as composed and published. However, the piece becomes a bit long if all the repeats are played. If you do choose to play the repeats, you can add interest by adding ornamentation on the repeats. We have made editorial suggestions appropriate to Baroque style regarding articulations and dynamics. In variation 1, notice the slurred notes. The half notes in variation 1, primarily in the left hand, could be played slightly detached. In variation 2, notice that we have suggested that quarter notes of the left hand are to be slurred, which contrast in articulation to the music previously played. One can imagine a tempo slightly less slow than the one recorded on the companion recording, but make sure that the tempo you choose remains steady throughout the theme and both variations. Do not make the mistake of playing this beautiful music in an inappropriate romantic style.

JOHANN PACHELBEL
German composer and organist.
Born in Nuremburg, September 1, 1653;
died in Nuremburg, March 9, 1706.

Pachelbel has enjoyed a surge of popularity in the last century, not only with the popularity of his Canon in D, but also a re-discovery of his enormous output of vocal and choral music, chamber music, plus organ and various keyboard works. The composer demonstrated excellent abilities in music from an early age. Pachelbel received training from several famous organists before studying music at the University of Altdorf and then the Gymnasium Poeticum. From 1763 to the end of his life, Pachelbel served as organist in a series of positions for both secular and sacred venues in Vienna, Eisenach, Erfurt, Stuttgart, Gotha, and Nuremburg. Despite his heavy performing schedule, Pachelbel was quite prolific as a composer.

Sarabande in B-flat Major

The sarabande has its roots in the zarabanda, a fast and erotic dance from Mexico and Spain in the 16th century. In France, the zarabanda was transformed into a slow Baroque dance, the sarabande, essentially a highly expressive slow minuet. Baroque sarabandes tend to be either majestic or mournful, and are musically characterized by a dotted note on the second beat of a three beat measure. To achieve some style, we recommend that the quarter note downbeats should be played with some separation before beat 2, as if they are eighth notes followed by eighth rests. Notice the stylistic articulation we have recommended in the right hand for beats 2 and 3. Sustain the chord on beat 2 until a *staccato* chord on the "and" of beat 3. Also, notice the articulation we have recommended in the left hand, with the slur to a *staccato* on beat 3. This is a simple piece of music, but if one applies stylistic articulation it becomes a challenge to maintain independent articulation between the hands. Do not make the mistake of applying romantic style to this lush little piece. Tempo, as always, is open for interpretation. One can imagine a slightly faster, more dance-like tempo than on the companion recording.

CHRISTIAN PETZOLD

German organist and composer.
Born in Königstein, 1677;
died in Dresden, 1733.

Only a little of the music by one of the seventeenth century's greatest organ players survives. Were it not for the two popular minuets copied into the *Notebook for Anna Magdelena Bach*, Petzold might be completely forgotten today. Very little is known of his life apart from various concerts around Europe, where he was featured as organist. He held a court position in Dresden, where he played and taught some of the great organists of the next generation.

Johann Sebastian Bach included the following pieces (BWV Appendix 114 and 115) in the second volume, dated 1725, of the *Notebook for Anna Magdalena Bach*. The notebooks (the first was begun in 1722) were for Bach's second wife, Anna Magdalena, who was much younger than the composer. Such keyboard notebooks of assembled favorite pieces were common in Baroque homes, and used for family music-making. (They are the equivalent of the modern published music collection, such as this one.) Some of the pieces in the Anna Magdalena notebook are by J.S. Bach; others are not. Previously attributed to Bach, we now know that the two pieces below are by Christian Petzold.

Minuet in G Major, BWV Appendix 114

We have no tempo from the composer for this famous minuet. The tempo on the companion recording is an excellent place to begin. In playing a minuet, do not forget its dance origins. This is an elegant and restrained dance that should remain steady throughout. There are many theories about how to articulate Baroque music, since composers of this period generally did not notate articulation and were not writing for a modern piano. We have made editorial suggestions in this edition that are one interpretation of how to achieve some Baroque style. The ornamentation in measures 3, 5, and 30 might be reserved for the repeats of these sections. You will notice on the companion recording some added ornamentation on the repeats, which is part of the style of this period. These added ornamentations are optional. This minuet should be played without pedal. Do not take the tempo too quickly.

Minuet in G minor, BWV Appendix 115

In playing a minuet in the Baroque, do not forget its dance origins. This is an elegant and restrained dance that should remain steady throughout. We have made editorial suggestions regarding articulations that may help to create Baroque style. A minor key minuet such as this one has a contemplative quality. We urge you not to take it too slowly. You will notice on the companion recording some added ornamentation on the repeats, which is part of the style of this period. These added ornamentations are optional. This minuet should be played without pedal. In general, the quarter notes of the left hand should be played with slight detachment throughout.

ALESSANDRO SCARLATTI

Italian composer.
Born in Palermo, May 2, 1660;
died in Naples, October 22, 1725.

Alessandro Scarlatti (father to Domenico Scarlatti) is often called the father of the Neapolitan school of eighteenth century opera. Tradition tells us that Scarlatti studied with Carissimi in Rome, which gave him access to the musical Italian elite and earned him the post as Maestro di cappella for the court of the queen. He worked for the viceroy of Naples and then for the Medici family in Florence. Scarlatti eventually returned to Naples after some time in Rome and Venice. Here his operas had fallen out of fashion and Scarlatti attempted to get commissions elsewhere, writing choral works until his death. Largely remembered as a composer of opera, oratorio and other vocal forms, Scarlatti did write a few keyboard works.

Aria in D minor

Unlike his son Domenico Scarlatti (who wrote over 500 keyboard sonatas), composer Alessandro Scarlatti was known for his operas and vocal music. This beautiful minor key aria has most of the motion in the left hand. However, in a performance one must not forget that the melody is in the right hand and should be prominent. The left hand is a simple accompaniment. You must find the tempo that captures the serious tone of this music, but is neither too fast nor too slow. Slow minor key Baroque music is often about melancholy contemplation. The original score shows measures 1–8 and 17–27 as repeated. For this edition, we have chosen to write out the repeats and offer suggestions for ornamentation appropriate to the period. (In Baroque music, when a section is repeated, such ornamentation is expected in the style.) Practice slowly hands alone. In practicing the left hand listen for absolute steadiness and phrase, created with the slurs that we have suggested. Use no pedal! The right hand needs beautiful phrasing and tone. Imagine a soprano with the most beautiful voice in the world singing this melody in a sensitive, floating tone. In slow Baroque music, a trill sometimes stylistically can begin slowly and increase in speed. You can hear this demonstrated on the companion recording.

DOMENICO SCARLATTI

Italian composer and harpsichordist.
Born in Naples, October 26, 1685;
died in Madrid, July 23, 1757.

Domenico was one of two musical sons of Alessandro Scarlatti. Domenico was extraordinarily influential in the development of solo keyboard music, composing nearly 600 sonatas for the instrument. He was taught by his father and other musicians in Naples until he secured the position of composer and organist for the royal chapel in Naples at the age of 15. He spent time in Venice and Rome serving as the Maestro di cappella at St. Peter's before moving to Lisbon, where he taught the Portuguese Princess. In 1728, he moved to Spain where he would spend the rest of his life, finally settling in Madrid. In Madrid he was the music master for the Princess and later Queen of Spain.

Minuet from Sonata in C Major, L. 217 (K. 73b, P. 80)

Domenico Scarlatti wrote more than 500 sonatas for keyboard. These sonatas rarely include a minuet. A minuet needs gracefulness and a steady rhythm. Remember its roots as dance music. We have made editorial recommendations about slurring, *staccato* and dynamics that may help you find some Baroque style in your performance. Do not make the mistake of playing this piece all with *legato* fingers, which will be completely inappropriate for Baroque style. Notice the echo effect in measures 14–17. The trills should be added only in the second time through both sections. They should always begin on the note above and on the beat. This is also true of the final trill in the last measure. Tempo is open for interpretation. One can imagine a tempo slightly slower than that on the companion recording.

GEORG PHILIPP TELEMANN

German composer.
Born in Magdeburg, March 14, 1681;
died in Hamburg, June 25, 1767.

A prominent German Baroque composer, Telemann was instrumental in expanding figured bass composition and defining Baroque ornamentation. He is sometimes cited as the most prolific composer who ever lived, with over 3,000 known music works, including about 150 keyboard pieces. He also wrote and published poetry. Telemann was a self-taught musician who held a series of positions in Leipzig, Sorau, Eisenach, Frankfurt, and finally Hamburg, where he became the music director of the city's churches.

Minuet from Suite in G Major, TWV 32:13

A minuet needs gracefulness and a steady rhythm. Remember its roots as dance music. In this period composers generally did not notate articulation details, and often did not mark dynamics. We have made editorial recommendations about slurring, *staccato* and dynamics that may help you find some Baroque style in your performance. Begin practice hands alone, playing slowly. Learn the articulations and dynamics from the beginning, along with the correct notes and rhythms. Then practice slowly hands together, retaining the articulation and dynamics you have been practicing hands separately. Gradually increase the speed over your weeks of practice, but always retain a steady beat. We recommend no pedal in playing this minuet.

—Richard Walters, editor
Joshua Parman, assistant editor

Minuet
from Suite in G Major

Georg Philipp Telemann
TWV 32:13

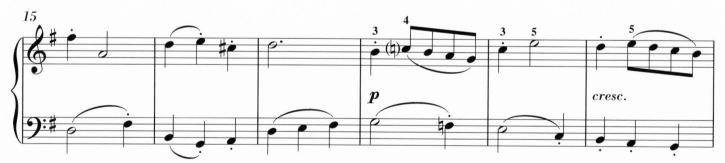

Fingering by Elena Abend.
Tempo, articulations, and dynamics are stylistic editorial suggestions.

Sonatina in C Major

William Duncombe

Allegretto

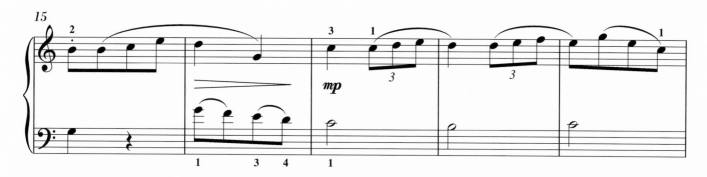

Fingering by Matthew Edwards.
Tempo, articulations and dynamics are stylistic editorial suggestions.

Minuet in G Major

attributed to Christian Petzold
BWV Appendix 114

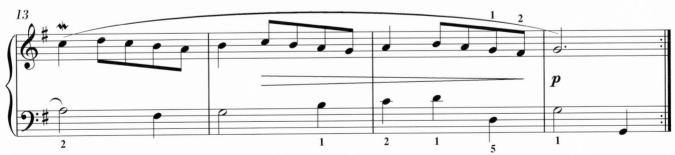

Edited and with fingering by Christos Tsitsaros.
Tempo, articulations and dynamics are editorial suggestions.

LABORUM
DULCE
LENIMEN

G. SCHIRMER

Minuet in F Major

George Frideric Handel

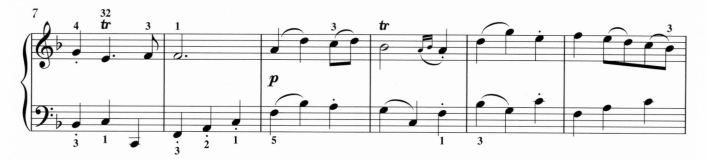

Fingering by Stefanie Jacob.
Tempo, articulations and dynamics are stylistic editorial suggestions. Trills begin on the note above.

Minuet in G minor

attributed to Christian Petzold
BWV Appendix 115

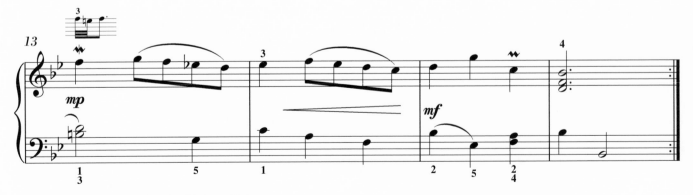

Edited and with fingering by Christos Tsitsaros.
Tempo, articulations and dynamics are editorial suggestions.

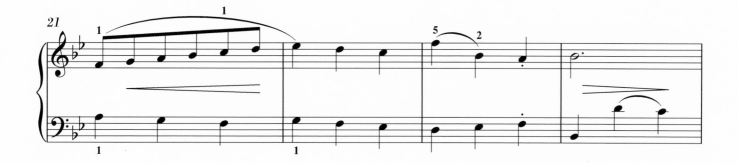

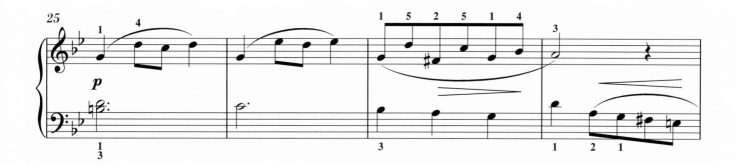

Courante in C Major

John Blow

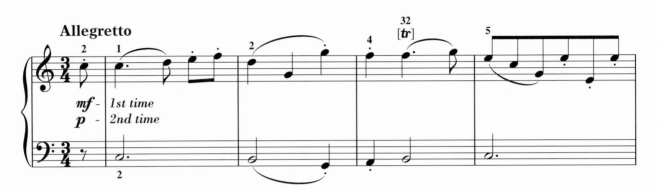

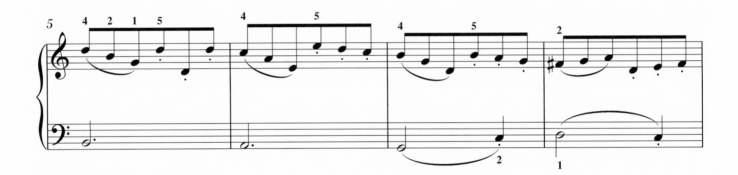

Fingering by Elena Abend.
Tempo, dynamics, and articulations are stylistic editorial suggestions. Trills begin on the note above.

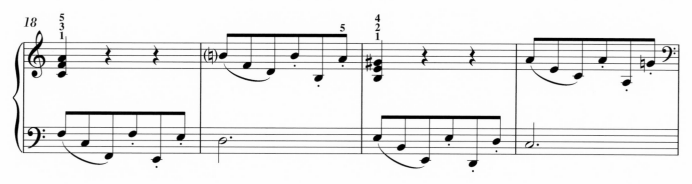

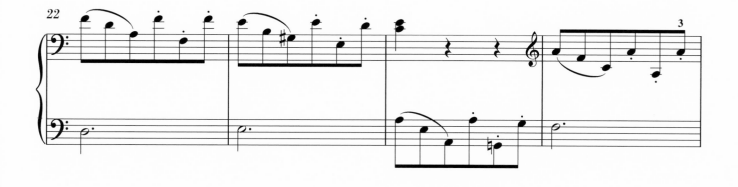

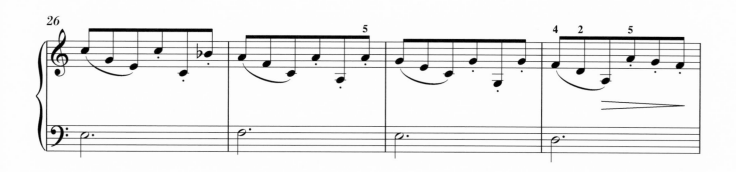

Rigaudon in G Major

George Frideric Handel

l.h. slightly detached throughout

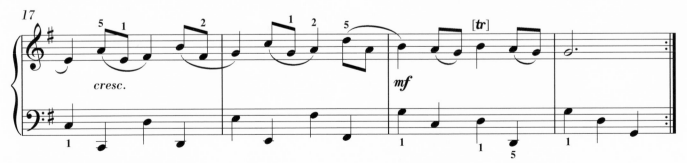

Fingering by Stefanie Jacob.
Tempo, articulations, and dynamics are stylistic editorial suggestions. Trills begin on the note above.

Impertinence
(Bourrée)

George Frideric Handel
HWV 494

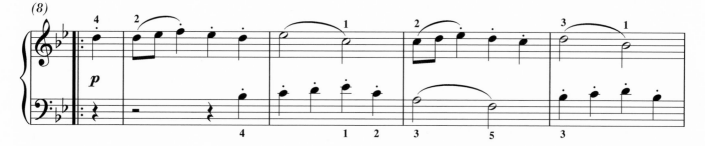

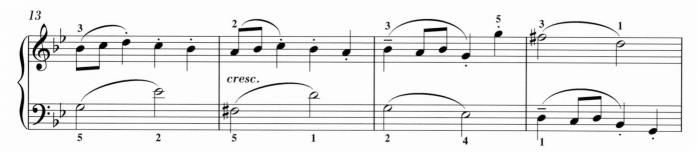

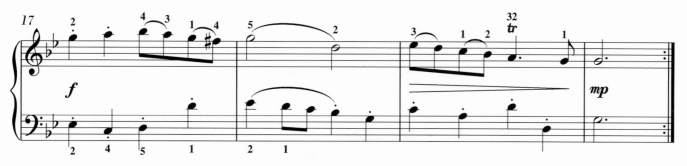

Fingering by Stefanie Jacob.
Tempo, articulations, and dynamics are stylistic editorial suggestions. Trills begin on the note above.

Musette in D Major

Composer unknown
BWV Appendix 126

Moderato

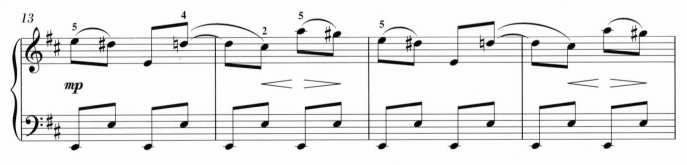

Edited and with fingering by Christos Tsitsaros.
Tempo, articulations and dynamics are editorial suggestions.

Minuet in D minor

Composer unknown
BWV Appendix 132

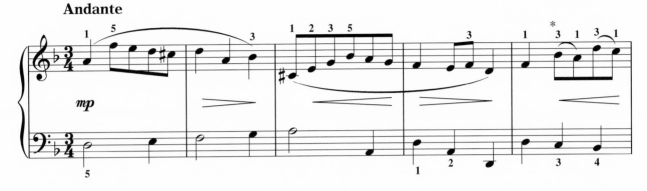

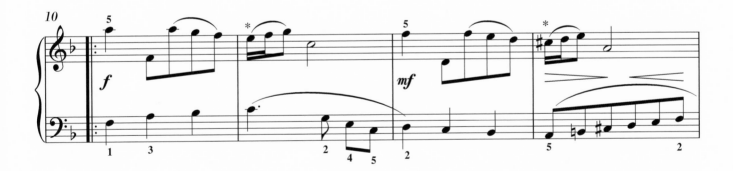

Edited and with fingering by Christos Tsitsaros.
*These slurs appear in the source manuscript. Other slurs are editorial sugestions.
Tempo, articulations and dynamics are editorial suggestions.

Minuet in G Major

Composer unknown
BWV Appendix 116

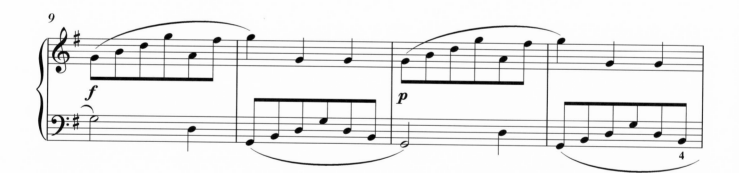

Edited and with fingering by Christos Tsitsaros.
Tempo, articulations and dynamics are editorial suggestions.

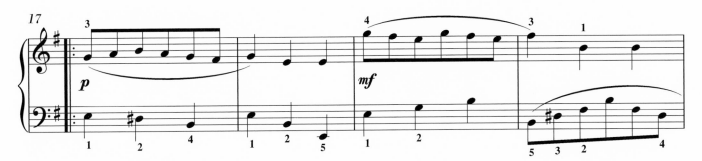

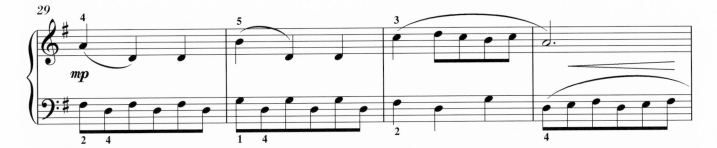

March in D Major

attributed to Carl Philipp Emanuel Bach
BWV Appendix 122

Edited and with fingering by Christos Tsitsaros.
Tempo, articulations and dynamics are editorial suggestions.

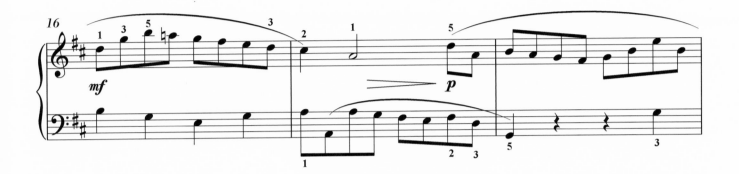

Sarabande in B-flat Major

Johann Pachelbel

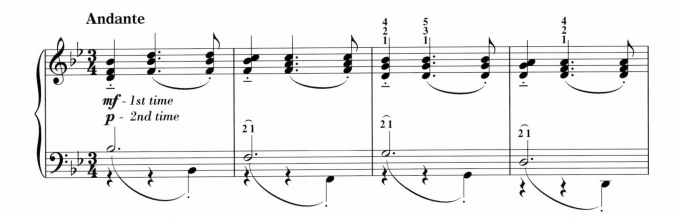

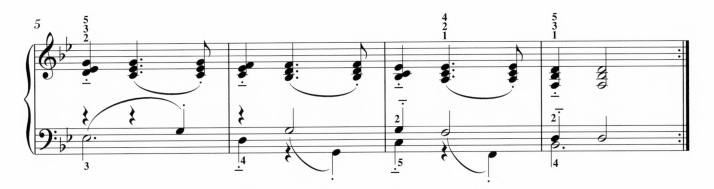

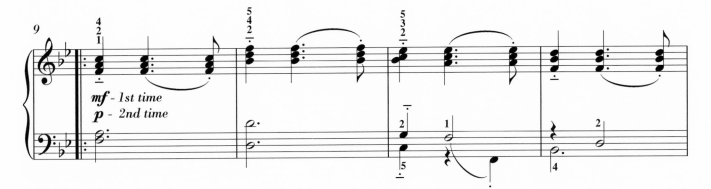

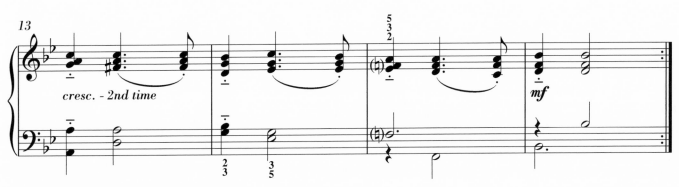

Fingering by Matthew Edwards.
Tempo, articulations, and dynamics are stylistic editorial suggestions.

Aria in D minor

Alessandro Scarlatti

Fingering by Jeannie Yu.
Articulations and dynamics are stylistic editorial suggestions. Suggested ornamentation has been notated in measures 9–16, 28–33. Trills begin on the note above.

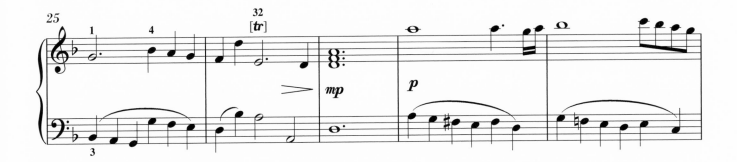

Sarabande
from Suite in D minor

George Frideric Handel
HWV 437

Larghetto

Fingering by Stefanie Jacob.
Tempo, articulations, and dynamics are editorial suggestions.

VAR. 1

VAR. 2

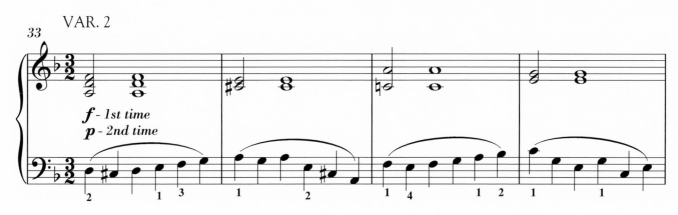

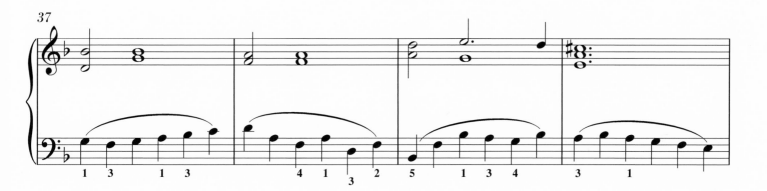

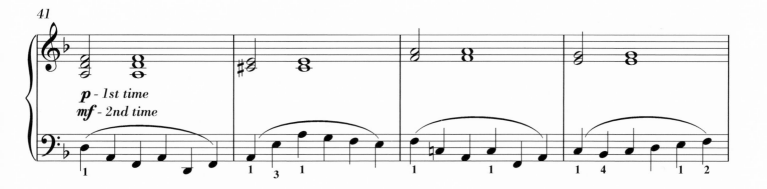

Minuet
from Sonata in C Major

Domenico Scarlatti
L. 217 (K. 73b, P. 80)

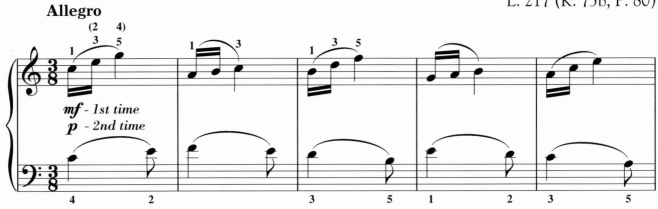

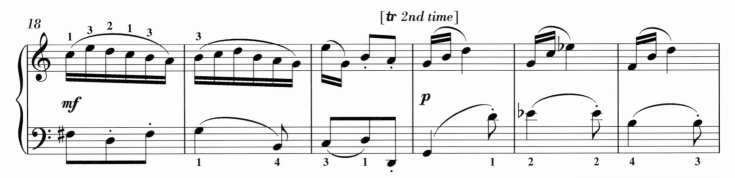

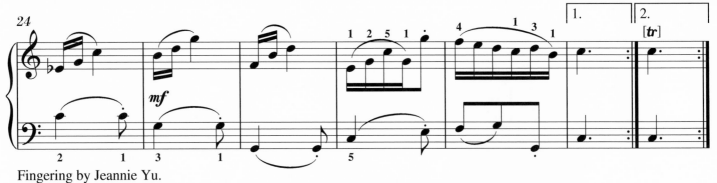

Fingering by Jeannie Yu.
Tempo, articulations and dynamics are stylistic editorial suggestions. Trills begin on the note above.

Benevolent Cuckoos Under Yellow Dominos

from *French Follies, or Costumes at a Masked Ball*

from the thirteenth order of Harpsichord Pieces, Book 1

François Couperin

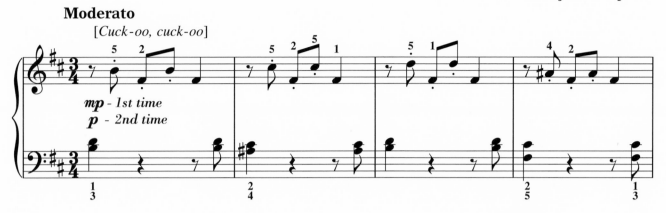

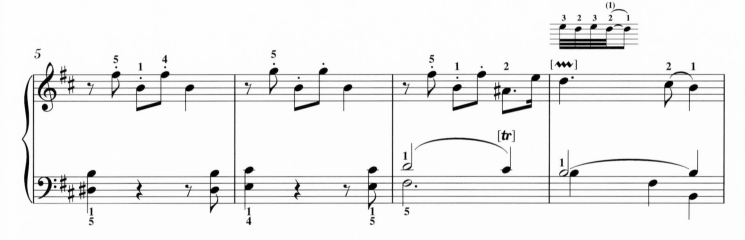

Fingering by Jeannie Yu.

Originally in $\frac{3}{8}$. Tempo, articulation and dynamics are stylistic editorial suggestions. Trills begin on the note above.

Berceuse
(Les graces-naturéles)
from the eleventh order of Harpsichord Pieces, Book 2

François Couperin

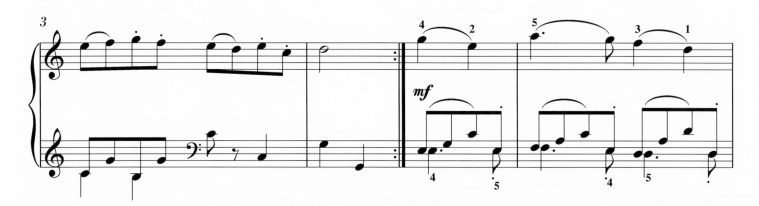

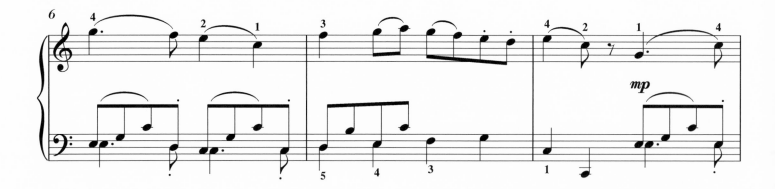

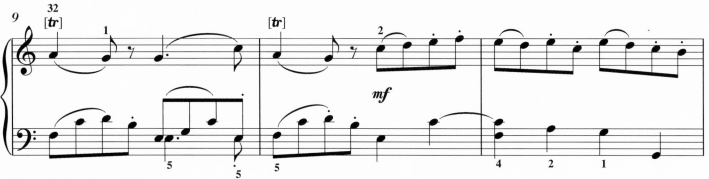

Fingering by Jeannie Yu.
Tempo, articulations and dynamics are stylistic editorial suggestions. Trills begin on the note above.

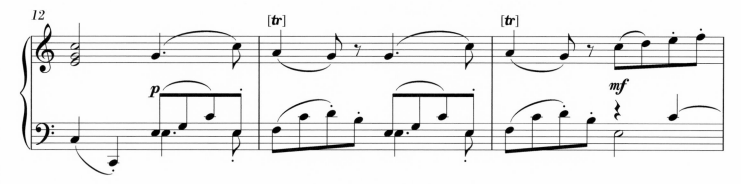

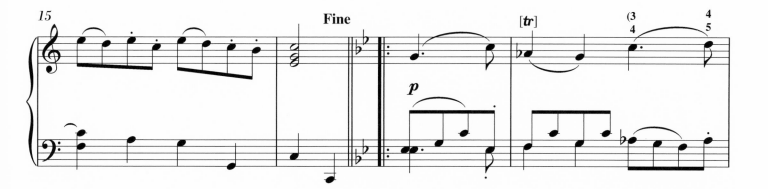

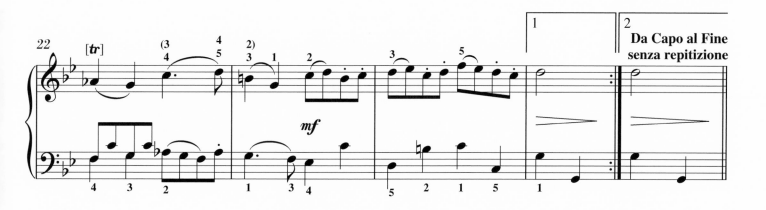

The Cuckoo
(Le Coucou)
from Harpsichord Pieces, Book 3

Louis-Claude Daquin

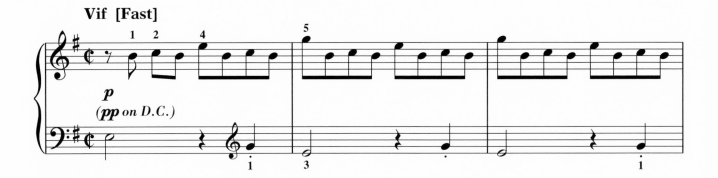

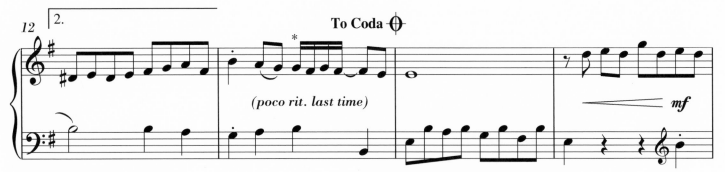

Fingering by Elena Abend.

Articulations and dynamics are stylistic editorial suggestions. Ornamentation has been notated for this edition in places marked with *. The original notation was in 2/4, changed in this edition to 2/2.

D.C. al Coda
(with repeat)

CODA

Prelude in C Major

John Blow

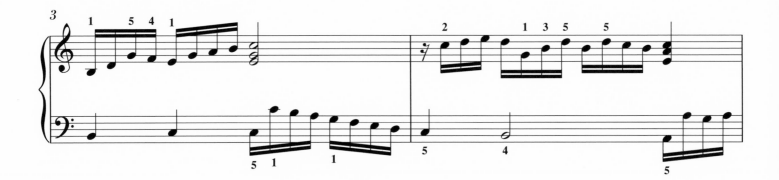

left hand quarter notes and half notes slightly detached

Fingering by Elena Abend.
Tempo and dynamics are stylistic editorial suggestions. Trills begin on the note above.

ABOUT THE EDITOR

RICHARD WALTERS

Richard Walters is a pianist, composer, and editor of hundred of publications in a long music publishing career. He is Vice President of Classical Publications at Hal Leonard, and directs a variety of publications for piano, voice, and solo instruments. Walters directs all publishing in the Schirmer Performance Editions series. Among other piano publications, he is editor of the revised edition of *Samuel Barber: Complete Piano Music, Leonard Bernstein: Music for Piano*, and the multi-volume series *The World's Great Classical Music*. His editing credits for vocal publications include *Samuel Barber: 65 Songs, Benjamin Britten: Collected Songs, Benjamin Britten: Complete Folksong Arrangements, Leonard Bernstein: Art Songs and Arias, The Purcell Collection: Realizations by Benjamin Britten, Bernstein Theatre Songs, G. Schirmer Collection of American Art Song, 28 Italian Songs and Arias for the Seventeenth and Eighteenth Centuries*, 80 volumes of standard repertoire in the Vocal Library series, and the multi-volume *The Singer's Musical Theatre Anthology*. Walters has published dozens of various arrangements, particularly for voice and piano, and is the composer of nine song cycles. He was educated with a bachelor's degree in piano at Simpson College, where he studied piano with Robert Larsen and composition with Sven Lekberg, and graduate studies in composition at the University of Minnesota, where he studied with Dominick Argento.